SURE

SIGNS

TED KOOSER

SURE SIGNS

New and Selected Poems

UNIVERSITY OF PITTSBURGH PRESS

Published by the University of Pittsburgh Press, Pittsburgh, Pa. 15261
Manufactured in the United States of America

10   9

Library of Congress Cataloging in Publication Data

Kooser, Ted.
  Sure signs.

  (Pitt poetry series)
  I. Title.
PS3561.06S9   811'.5'4   79-21725
ISBN 0-8229-3410-8
ISBN 0-8229-5313-7 pbk.

A CIP catalogue record for this book is available from the British Library.

Some of these poems have appeared in the following periodicals: *American Poetry Review,* *Bits, The Berkeley Monthly, Cottonwood Review, Crazy Horse, Dacotah Territory, December, Field, Great Granny Press Postcard Series, Hearse, The Lamp in the Spine, Midwest Quarterly, The Nation, Pebble, Periodical of Art in Nebraska, Plainsong, Poet & Critic, Poetry Now, Raccoon, Rapport, The Reporter, The Small Farm, South Dakota Review, Southern Poetry Review,* and *Thistle.*

Others have appeared in the following books: *Cottonwood County* (Windflower Press), *Grass County* (Windflower Press), *A Local Habitation & a Name* (Solo Press), *Not Coming to Be Barked At* (Pentagram Press), *Official Entry Blank* (University of Nebraska Press), *So This Is Nebraska/Shooting a Farmhouse* (Ally Press), and *Twenty Poems by Ted Kooser* (Best Cellar Press.)

"There Is Always a Little Wind," originally published as "Small Country Poem," first appeared in *Blue Moon News,* copyright © 1976 by *Blue Moon Press* Inc. "The Salesman" originally appeared in *Poetry Northwest,* 20, no. 1 (Spring 1979). "Late September," "Visiting Mountains," and "Walking Beside a Creek" first appeared in *Prairie Schooner,* copyright 1975 by University of Nebraska Press. "Carrie," "The Man with the Hearing Aid," and "An Old Photograph" first appeared in *Prairie Schooner,* copyright 1978 by University of Nebrask Press. "Five P.M." originally appeared in *Scree.* "The Constellation Orion," "The Afterlife," "Book Club," and "A Summer Night" first appeared in *Three Rivers Poetry Journal,* copyright © 1975, 1976, 1980.

"The Goldfish Floats to the Top of His Life," "A Place in Kansas," and "The Blind Always Come as Such a Surprise" are reprinted from *Heartland II: Poets of the Midwest,* copyright © 1975 by Northern Illinois University Press. Reprinted by permission of the publisher. "August," "Fort Robinson," "Late February," and "Sitting All Evening Alone in the Kitchen" appeared originally in volume VI of *Voyages to the Inland Sea* (University of Wisconsin — La Crosse: Center for Contemporary Poetry, 1976).

A number of these poems were written with the encouragement of a fellowship from the Literature Program of the National Endowment for the Arts.

The publication of this book is supported by grants from the National Endowment for the Arts in Washington, D.C., a Federal agency, and the Pennsylvania Council on the Arts.

for Kathy

CONTENTS

SURE
SIGNS

SELECTING A READER

First, I would have her be beautiful,
and walking carefully up on my poetry
at the loneliest moment of an afternoon,
her hair still damp at the neck
from washing it. She should be wearing
a raincoat, an old one, dirty
from not having money enough for the cleaners.
She will take out her glasses, and there
in the bookstore, she will thumb
over my poems, then put the book back
up on its shelf. She will say to herself,
"For that kind of money, I can get
my raincoat cleaned." And she will.

FIRST SNOW

The old black dog comes in one evening
with the first few snowflakes on his back
and falls asleep, throwing his bad leg out
at our excitement. This is the night
when one of us gets to say, as if it were news,
that no two snowflakes are ever alike;
the night when each of us remembers something
snowier. The kitchen is a kindergarten
steamy with stories. The dog gets stiffly up
and limps away, seeking a quiet spot
at the heart of the house. Outside,
in silence, with diamonds in his fur,
the winter night curls round the legs of the trees,
sleepily blinking snowflakes from his lashes.

AN OLD PHOTOGRAPH

This old couple, Nils and Lydia,
were married for seventy years.
Here they are sixty years old
and already like brother
and sister—small, lustreless eyes,
large ears, the same serious line
to the mouths. After those years
spent together, sharing
the weather of sex, the sour milk
of lost children, barns burning,
grasshoppers, fevers and silence,
they were beginning to share
their hard looks. How far apart
they sit; not touching at shoulder
or knee, hands clasped in their laps
as if under each pair was a key
to a trunk hidden somewhere,
full of those lessons one keeps
to himself.
        They had probably
risen at daybreak, and dressed
by the stove, Lydia wearing
black wool with a collar of lace,
Nils his worn suit. They had driven
to town in the wagon and climbed
to the studio only to make
this stern statement, now veined
like a leaf, that though they looked
just alike they were separate people,
with separate wishes already
gone stale, a good two feet of space
between them, thirty years to go.

THE CONSTELLATION ORION

I'm delighted to see you,
old friend,
lying there in your hammock
over the next town.
You were the first person
my son was to meet in the heavens.
He's sleeping now,
his head like a small sun in my lap.
Our car whizzes along in the night.
If he were awake, he'd say,
"Look, Daddy, there's Old Ryan!"
but I won't wake him.
He's mine for the weekend,
Old Ryan, not yours.

THE SALESMAN

Today he's wearing his vinyl shoes,
shiny and white as little Karmann Ghias
fresh from the body shop, and as he moves
in his door-to-door glide, these shoes fly round
each other, honking the horns of their soles.
His hose are black and ribbed and tight, as thin
as an old umbrella or the wing of a bat.
(They leave a pucker when he pulls them off.)
He's got on his double-knit leisure suit
in a pond-scum green, with a tight white belt
that matches his shoes but suffers with cracks
at the golden buckle. His shirt is brown
and green, like a pile of leaves, and it opens
onto the neck at a Brillo pad
of graying hair which tosses a cross and chain
as he walks. The collar is splayed out over
the jacket's lapels yet leaves a lodge pin
taking the sun like a silver spike.
He's swinging a briefcase full of the things
of this world, a leather cornucopia
heavy with promise. Through those dark lenses,
each of the doors along your sunny street
looks slightly ajar, and in your quiet house
the dog of your willpower cowers and growls,
then crawls in under the basement steps,
making the jingle of coin with its tags.

OLD SOLDIERS' HOME

On benches in front of the Old Soldiers' Home,
the old soldiers unwrap the pale brown packages
of their hands, folding the fingers back
and looking inside, then closing them up again
and gazing off across the grounds,
safe with the secret.

SELF-PORTRAIT AT THIRTY-NINE

A barber is cutting the hair;
his fingers, perfumed by a rainbow
of bottled oils, blanket the head
with soft, pink clouds. Through these,
the green eyes, from their craters, peer.

There's a grin lost somewhere
in the folds of the face, with a fence
of old teeth, broken and leaning,
through which asides to the barber
pounce catlike onto the air.

This is a face which shows its age,
has all of the coin it started with,
with the look of having been counted
too often. Oh, but I love
my face! It is that hound of bronze

who faithfully stands by the door
to hold it open wide—on light,
on water, on leafy streets
where women pass it with a smile.
Good dog, old face; good dog, good dog.

CHRISTMAS EVE

Now my father carries his old heart
in its basket of ribs
like a child coming into the room
with an injured bird.
Our ages sit down with a table between them,
eager to talk.
Our common bones are wrapped in new robes.
A common pulse tugs at the ropes
in the backs of our hands.
We are so much alike
we both weep at the end of his stories.

AUGUST

The cicada shell
clings to a day in the past,
its broken lantern
dusty with evening light.

Walking alone toward the house,
my life is a moon
in the frail blue branches
of my veins.

AT THE BUS STOP
NEXT TO THE FUNERAL HOME

At the bus stop next to the funeral home,
a man in galoshes is sweeping the grass
with a metal detector. The empty buses
rock past wheezing, holding the stiff silver poles
of their headlights before them. The man looms up
in white shirt, earphones, his spectacles
mirrors—a moth of a man, the proboscis
sucking for dimes in the satiny
funeral shadow. Behind him, the building
is Cadillac black, except for one light
leaking through fan blades close to the ground,
hidden in yews. Now the man stoops,
picks something out of the grass and holds it
up to the moon. Whatever it is,
it's enough; he pockets it quickly and turns
to a door opening out of the shrubs,
a dim staircase descending beyond it.
The door closes behind him. All night,
the buses rock past with no one aboard,
and the fan in the little basement window
chops up the light with its squeal.

VISITING MOUNTAINS

The plains ignore us,
but these mountains listen,
an audience of thousands
holding its breath
in each rock. Climbing,
we pick our way
over the skulls of small talk.
On the prairies below us,
the grass leans this way and that
in discussion;
words fly away like corn shucks
over the fields.
Here, lost in a mountain's
attention, there's nothing to say.

THE LEAKY FAUCET

All through the night, the leaky faucet
searches the stillness of the house
with its radar blip: who is awake?
Who lies out there as full of worry
as a pan in the sink? *Cheer up,*
cheer up, the little faucet calls,
someone will help you through your life.

THE SOUL OF TWINS

for Jonathan Holden

The single soul of a pair of twins
is a man who feels as if two strangers
were walking away with the halves
of his heart. Wherever they take him,
two sorrows in old carpet slippers
show him up to his rooms and pull
the cracked shades. In the still pallor
of dawn, two voices call out sharply
into their echoes. But once each year,
on his birthday, they bring him home
and put him together again
in his mother's kitchen. He's at peace
at her side, helping with dishes
and watching the two red suns go down
behind the slack swings in the schoolyard.

A FROZEN STREAM

This snake has gone on,
all muscle and glitter,
into the woods,
a few leaves clinging,
red, yellow, and brown.
Oh, how he sparkled!
The roots of the old trees
gleamed as he passed.

Now there is nothing
to see; an old skin
caught in the bushes,
bleached and flaking,
a few sharp stones
already poking through.

LIVING NEAR
THE REHABILITATION HOME

Tonight she is making her way
up the block by herself, throwing
her heavy shoes from step to step,
her lunchbox swinging out wide
with a rhythmical clunk, each bone
on its end and feebly bending
into her pitiful gait. Where is
her friend tonight, the idiot boy?
Each day at this time I see them
walking together, his bright red jacket
trying the dusk, her old blue coat
his shadow. She moves too slowly
for him, and he breaks from her hand
and circles her in serious orbits,
stamping his feet in the grass.
Perhaps they have taken him elsewhere
to live. From high on my good legs
I imagine her lonely without him,
but perhaps she's happy at last.

LATE FEBRUARY

The first warm day,
and by mid-afternoon
the snow is no more
than a washing
strewn over the yards,
the bedding rolled in knots
and leaking water,
the white shirts lying
under the evergreens.
Through the heaviest drifts
rise autumn's fallen
bicycles, small carnivals
of paint and chrome,
the Octopus
and Tilt-A-Whirl
beginning to turn
in the sun. Now children,
stiffened by winter
and dressed, somehow,
like old men, mutter
and bend to the work
of building dams.

But such a spring is brief;
by five o'clock
the chill of sundown,
darkness, the blue TVs
flashing like storms
in the picture windows,
the yards gone gray,
the wet dogs barking
at nothing. Far off
across the cornfields
staked for streets and sewers,
the body of a farmer
missing since fall
will show up
in his garden tomorrow,
as unexpected
as a tulip.

A DRIVE IN THE COUNTRY

In the ditch by the dirt back road
late in March, a few black snowdrifts
lie in the grass like old men
asleep in their coats. It's the dirt
of the road that has kept them
so cold at the heart. We drive by
without stopping for them.

SPRING PLOWING

West of Omaha the freshly plowed fields
steam in the night like lakes.
The smell of the earth floods over the roads.
The field mice are moving their nests
to the higher ground of fence rows,
the old among them crying out to the owls
to take them all. The paths in the grass
are loud with the squeak of their carts.
They keep their lanterns covered.

SITTING ALL EVENING ALONE
IN THE KITCHEN

The cat has fallen asleep,
the dull book of a dead moth
loose in his paws.

The moon in the window, the tide
gurgling out through the broken shells
in the old refrigerator.

Late, I turn out the lights.
The little towns on top of the stove
glow faintly neon,
sad women alone at the bar.

SURE SIGNS

for George Von Glahn

So many crickets tonight—
like strings of sleigh bells!
"A long hard winter ahead
for sure," my neighbor says,
reeling a cobweb onto
a broom in his garden.
"Crickets and cobwebs," he says,
"sure signs. In seventy years
(he looks out over his glasses
to see if I'm still there)
you get to know a thing or two."

THE SKELETON IN THE CLOSET

These bones once held together
on the strength of rumor.
The jaws which bit down hard
on the truth were stuffed at last
with a velvet glove. Now
all that foolishness is dust
and mothballs and the eyes
of children darkening
the keyhole. There's nothing
to see in here but two boots
full of golden teeth
and a fancy riding cape
with shoulder pads.

A SUMMER NIGHT

At the end of the street
a porch light is burning,
showing the way. How simple,
how perfect it seems: the darkness,
the white house like a passage
through summer and into
a snowfield. Night after night,
the lamp comes on at dusk,
the end of the street
stands open and white,
and an old woman sits there
tending the lonely gate.

IN A COUNTRY CEMETERY IN IOWA

for James Hearst

Someone's been up here nights,
and in a hurry,
breaking the headstones.

And someone else,
with a little time to spare,
has mended them;

some farmer, I'd say,
who knows his welding.
He's stacked them up in

harnesses of iron,
old angle iron and strap,
taking a little extra time

to file the welds down smooth.
Just passing through, you'd say
it looks like foolishness.

THE MAN WITH THE HEARING AID

A man takes out his hearing aid
and falls asleep, his good ear deep
in the pillow. Thousands of bats
fly out of the other ear.
All night they flutter and dive
through laughter, catching the punch lines,
their ears all blood and velvet.
At dawn they return. The weary squeaks
make the old stone cavern ring
with gibberish. As the man awakens,
the last of the bats folds into sleep.
His ear is thick with fur and silence.

THE VERY OLD

The very old are forever
hurting themselves,

burning their fingers
on skillets, falling

loosely as trees
and breaking their hips

with muffled explosions of bone.
Down the block

they are wheeled in
out of our sight

for years at a time.
To make conversation,

the neighbors ask
if they are still alive.

Then, early one morning,
through our kitchen windows

we see them again,
first one and then another,

out in their gardens
on crutches and canes,

perennial,
checking their gauges for rain.

WALKING BESIDE A CREEK

Walking beside a creek
in December, the black ice
windy with leaves,
you can feel the great joy
of the trees, their coats
thrown open like drunken men,
the lifeblood thudding
in their tight, wet boots.

BOOK CLUB

Mother has come to the clean end
of a morning full of the clink of mints
in little dishes, of lemon oil
tart in the living-room air,
of the water ballet of the folding chairs
rehearsing their kicks in a circle
of patience. The ladies are due
at two o'clock, a fat tour guide
of Hawaii on schedule, lagoons
of romance to lap the hot shore
in each girdle, volcanoes of ashes
filling the ashtrays, the bright birds
of sweet smiles crisscrossing
the circle.
   Meanwhile, my father
is picking up leaves from the drive;
as he bends, his blood tries the loose doors
of his arteries. At sixty-six,
with his retirement Bulova
wound tight as his heart, he has entered
the blue, high-altitude hallway of age.
There air is thin. If he looks forward
or back he gets dizzy. Today, in the bleak
exile of book club, even his bathroom's
forbidden to him. His razor and soap
have been hidden, his pills put away.

If he needs to go to the bathroom,
he'll have to walk down to the station
and ask for the key. Most likely though,
he's safe.
          At the foot of the stairs
to the basement, he's drawn up an armchair
and floor lamp. Through the long afternoon,
he'll sit there pretending to read,
while above him the pink mints go around
in slow circles, and lovely Hawaii
comes to Des Moines in the hula
of numb fannies on laboring chairs.

AT THE END OF THE WEEKEND

It is Sunday afternoon,
and I suddenly miss
my distant son, who at ten
has just this instant buzzed
my house in a flying
cardboard box, dipping
one wing to look down over
my shimmering roof, the yard,
the car in the drive. In his room
three hundred miles from me,
he tightens his helmet,
grips the controls, turns
loops and rolls. My windows
rattle. On days like this,
the least quick shadow crossing
the page makes me look up
at the sky like a goose,
squinting to see that flash
that I dream is his thought of me
daring to fall through the distance,
then climbing, full throttle, away.

UNCLE ADLER

He had come to the age
when his health had put cardboard
in all of its windows.
The oil in his eyes was so old
it would barely light,
and his chest was a chimney
full of bees. Of it all,
he had nothing to say;
his Adam's apple hung like a ham
in a stairwell. Lawyers
encircled the farm like a fence,
and his daughters fought over
the china. Then one day
while everyone he'd ever loved
was digging in his yard,
he suddenly sucked in his breath so hard
the whole estate fell in on him.

IN THE CORNERS OF FIELDS

Something is calling to me
from the corners of fields,
where the leftover fence wire
suns its loose coils, and stones
thrown out of the furrow
sleep in warm litters;
where the gray faces
of old No Hunting signs
mutter into the wind,
and dry horse tanks
spout fountains of sunflowers;
where a moth
flutters in from the pasture,
harried by sparrows,
and alights on a post,
so sure of its life
that it peacefully opens its wings.

HOW TO MAKE RHUBARB WINE

Go to the patch some afternoon
in early summer, fuzzy with beer
and sunlight, and pick a sack
of rhubarb (red or green will do)
and God knows watch for rattlesnakes
or better, listen; they make a sound
like an old lawn mower rolled downhill.
Wear a hat. A straw hat's best
for the heat but lets the gnats in.
Bunch up the stalks and chop the leaves off
with a buck knife and be careful.
You need ten pounds; a grocery bag
packed full will do it. Then go home
and sit barefooted in the shade
behind the house with a can of beer.
Spread out the rhubarb in the grass
and wash it with cold water
from the garden hose, washing
your feet as well. Then take a nap.
That evening, dice the rhubarb up
and put it in a crock. Then pour
eight quarts of boiling water in,
cover it up with a checkered cloth
to keep the fruit flies out of it,
and let it stand five days or so.
Take time each day to think of it.

Ferment ten days, under the cloth,
sniffing of it from time to time,
then siphon it off, swallowing some,
and bottle it. Sit back and watch
the liquid clear to honey yellow,
bottled and ready for the years,
and smile. You've done it awfully well.

LATE LIGHTS IN MINNESOTA

At the end of a freight train rolling away,
a hand swinging a lantern.
The only lights left behind in the town
are a bulb burning cold in the jail,
and high in one house,
a five-battery flashlight
pulling an old woman downstairs to the toilet
among the red eyes of her cats.

THE AFTERLIFE

It will be February there,
a foreign-language newspaper
rolling along the dock
in an icy wind, a few
old winos wiping their eyes
over a barrel of fire;
down the streets, mad women
shaking rats from their mops
on each stoop, and odd,
twisted children,
playing with matches and knives.
Then, behind us, trombones:
the horns of the tugs
turning our great gray ship
back into the mist.

A WIDOW

She's combed his neckties out of her hair
and torn out the tongues of his shoes.
She's poured his ashes out of their urn
and into his humidor. For the very last time,
she's scrubbed the floor around the toilet.
She hates him even more for dying.

SO THIS IS NEBRASKA

The gravel road rides with a slow gallop
over the fields, the telephone lines
streaming behind, its billow of dust
full of the sparks of redwing blackbirds.

On either side, those dear old ladies,
the loosening barns, their little windows
dulled by cataracts of hay and cobwebs
hide broken tractors under their skirts.

So this is Nebraska. A Sunday
afternoon; July. Driving along
with your hand out squeezing the air,
a meadowlark waiting on every post.

Behind a shelterbelt of cedars,
top-deep in hollyhocks, pollen and bees,
a pickup kicks its fenders off
and settles back to read the clouds.

You feel like that; you feel like letting
your tires go flat, like letting the mice
build a nest in your muffler, like being
no more than a truck in the weeds,

clucking with chickens or sticky with honey
or holding a skinny old man in your lap
while he watches the road, waiting
for someone to wave to. You feel like

waving. You feel like stopping the car
and dancing around on the road. You wave
instead and leave your hand out gliding
larklike over the wheat, over the houses.

FORT ROBINSON

When I visited Fort Robinson,
where Dull Knife and his Northern Cheyenne
were held captive that terrible winter,
the grounds crew was killing the magpies.

Two men were going from tree to tree
with sticks and ladders, poking the young birds
down from their nests and beating them to death
as they hopped about in the grass.

Under each tree where the men had worked
were twisted clots of matted feathers,
and above each tree a magpie circled,
crazily calling in all her voices.

We didn't get out of the car.
My little boy hid in the back and cried
as we drove away, into those ragged buttes
the Cheyenne climbed that winter, fleeing.

HOW TO FORETELL A CHANGE
IN THE WEATHER

Rain always follows the cattle
sniffing the air and huddling
in fields with their heads to the lee.
You will know that the weather is changing
when your sheep leave the pasture
too slowly, and your dogs lie about
and look tired; when the cat
turns her back to the fire,
washing her face, and the pigs
wallow in litter; cocks will be crowing
at unusual hours, flapping their wings;
hens will chant; when your ducks
and your geese are too noisy,
and the pigeons are washing themselves;
when the peacocks squall loudly
from the tops of the trees,
when the guinea fowl grates;
when sparrows chip loudly
and fuss in the roadway, and when swallows
fly low, skimming the earth;
when the carrion crow
croaks to himself, and wild fowl
dip and wash, and when moles
throw up hills with great fervor;
when toads creep out in numbers;
when frogs croak; when bats
enter the houses; when birds
begin to seek shelter,
and the robin approaches your house;
when the swan flies at the wind,
and your bees leave the hive;
when ants carry their eggs to and fro,
and flies bite, and the earthworm
is seen on the surface of things.

41

SNOW FENCE

The red fence
takes the cold trail
north; no meat
on its ribs,
but neither has it
much to carry.

IN AN OLD APPLE ORCHARD

The wind's an old man
to this orchard; these trees
have been feeling
the soft tug of his gloves
for a hundred years.
Now it's April again,
and again that old fool
thinks he's young.
He's combed the dead leaves
out of his beard; he's put on
perfume. He's gone off
late in the day
toward the town, and come back
slow in the morning,
reeling with bees.
As late as noon, if you look
in the long grass,
you can see him
still rolling about in his sleep.

AN EMPTY PLACE

There is nothing for Death
in an empty house,
nor left for him in the white dish
broken over the road.

Come and sit down by me
on the sunny stoop,
and let your heart so gently
rock you, rock you.

There is nothing to harm us here.

IN THE KITCHEN, AT MIDNIGHT

I snap on the light
and a cockroach
zips over the floor
like a skateboard
and without slowing down
skims under the door
to the cupboard,
becoming a can
of tomatoes. How
Ovid would love it!

Cockroach, wherever
you are, whatever
shape you've assumed,
I take you for
my model. I want to
eat poisons and live,
to breathe poisons
yet run like the wind,
to laugh my brown way
through thousands of years
of no cancer or wars
or Republicans, and,
once in a while,
in the night, I'd like
a light flashing on
like the bomb, if only
for memory's sake.

AFTER THE FUNERAL: CLEANING OUT
THE MEDICINE CABINET

Behind this mirror no new world
opens to Alice. Instead, we find
the old world, rearranged in rows,
a dusty little chronicle
of small complaints and private sorrows,
each cough caught dry and airless
in amber, the sore feet powdered
and cool in their yellow can.
To this world turned the burning eyes
after their search, the weary back
after its lifting, the heavy heart
like an old dog, sniffing the lids
for an answer. Now one of us
unscrews the caps and tries the air
of each disease. Another puts
the booty in a shoe box: tins
of laxatives and aspirin,
the corn pads and the razor blades,
while still another takes the vials
of secret sorrows—the little pills
with faded, lonely codes—holding
them out the way one holds a spider
pinched in a tissue, and pours them down
the churning toilet and away.

THE GRANDFATHER CAP

Sometimes I think that as he aged,
this cap, with the stain in its brim
like a range of dark mountains,
became the horizon to him.
He never felt right with it off.

SHOOTING A FARMHOUSE

The first few wounds are nearly invisible;
a truck rumbles past in the dust
and a .22 hole appears in the mailbox
like a fly landing there.
In a month you can see sky
through the tail of the windmill.
The attic windows grow black and uneasy.
When the last hen is found shot in the yard,
the old man and his wife move away.

In November, a Land Rover
flattens the gate like a tank
and pulls up in the yard. Hunters spill out
and throw down their pheasants like hats.
They blow out the rest of the windows,
set beer cans up on the porch rails
and shoot from the hip.
One of them walks up and yells in,
"Is anyone home?" getting a laugh.

By sunset, they've kicked down the door.
In the soft blush of light,
they blast holes in the plaster
and piss on the floors.

When the beer and the shells are all gone,
they drive sadly away,
the blare of their radio fading.
A breeze sighs in the shelterbelt.
Back in the house,
the newspapers left over from packing
the old woman's dishes
begin to blow back and forth through the rooms.

BEER BOTTLE

In the burned-
out highway
ditch the throw-

away beer
bottle lands
standing up

unbroken,
like a cat
thrown off

of a roof
to kill it,
landing hard

and dazzled
in the sun,
right side up;

sort of a
miracle.

SLEEPING CAT

My cat is asleep on his haunches
like a sphinx. He has gone down cautiously
into an earlier life, holding a thread
of the old world's noises, and feeling his way
through the bones. The scratch of my pen
keeps the thread taut. When I finish
the poem, and the sound in the room goes slack,
the cat will come scampering back
into the blinding, bright rooms of his eyes.

NORTH OF ALLIANCE

This is an empty house; not a stick
of furniture left, not even
a newspaper sodden with rain
under a broken window; nothing
to tell us the style of the people
who lived here, but that
they took it along. But wait:
here, penciled in inches
up a doorframe, these little marks
mark the growth of a child
impatient to get on with it,
a child stretching his neck
in a hurry to leave nothing here
but an absence grown tall in a doorway.

LATE SEPTEMBER

Behind each garage a ladder
sleeps in the leaves, its hands
folded across its lean belly.
There are hundreds of them
in each town, and more
sleeping by haystacks and barns
out in the country—tough old
day laborers, seasoned and wheezy,
drunk on the weather,
sleeping outside with the crickets.

CARRIE

"There's never an end to dust
and dusting," my aunt would say
as her rag, like a thunderhead,
scudded across the yellow oak
of her little house. There she lived
seventy years with a ball
of compulsion closed in her fist,
and an elbow that creaked and popped
like a branch in a storm. Now dust
is her hands and dust her heart.
There's never an end to it.

FOR A FRIEND

Late November, driving to Wichita.
A black veil of starlings
snags on a thicket and falls.
Shadows of wings skitter over
the highway, like leaves, like ashes.

You have been dead for six months;
though summer and fall
were lighter by one life,
they didn't seem to show it.
The seasons, those steady horses,
are used to the fickle weight
of our shifting load.

I'll guess how it was; on the road
through the wood, you stood up
in the back of the hangman's cart,
reached a low-hanging branch,
and swung up into the green leaves
of our memories.
    Old friend,
the stars were shattered windshield glass
for weeks; we all were sorry.

They never found that part of you
that made you drink, that made you cruel.
You knew we loved you anyway.

Black streak across the centerline,
all highways make me think of you.

GRANDFATHER

Driving the team, he came up over
the hill and looked down. In the white bowl
of the snow-covered valley, his house
was aflame like a wick, drawing up
into itself all that he'd worked for.

Once, forty years later, we passed.
It was October. The cellar
was filled by a flame of young trees.
I got out, but he sat in the back
and stared straight ahead, this old, old man,
still tight on the reins of his years.

LOOKING FOR YOU, BARBARA

I have been out looking for you,
Barbara, and as I drove around,
the steering wheel turned through my hands
like a clock. The moon
rolled over the rooftops and was gone.

I was dead tired; in my arms
they were rolling the tires inside;
in my legs they were locking the pumps.
Yet what was in me for you
flapped as red in my veins
as banners strung over a car lot.

Then I came home and got drunk.
Where were you? 2 A.M.
is full of slim manikins
waving their furs from black windows.
My bed goes once more around the block,
and my heart keeps on honking its horn.

POCKET POEM

If this comes creased and creased again and soiled
as if I'd opened it a thousand times
to see if what I'd written here was right,
it's all because I looked for you too long
to put it in your pocket. Midnight says
the little gifts of loneliness come wrapped
by nervous fingers. What I wanted this
to say was that I want to be so close
that when you find it, it is warm from me.

MOLES

The young of the mole
are born in the skull of a mayor.
They learn *footfall*
and *rain*. In the Season
of Falling Pinecones, they gather
in churches of ribs,
whining and puking.
When one of the old moles dies,
the young push him out of his tunnel
and set him afloat on the light.
This is the way we find them
out in the garden,
their little oars
pulled up and drying.

NOTES ON THE DEATH
OF NELS PAULSSEN, FARMER,
AT THE RIPE OLD AGE OF 93

A harvest
of nail parings,

a wagonload
of hair—

over his ashen
fields,

no dust
in the air.

ADVICE

We go out of our way to get home,
getting lost in a rack of old clothing,
fainting in stairwells,
our pulses fluttering like moths.
We will always be
leaving our loves like old stoves
in abandoned apartments. Early in life
there are signals of how it will be—
we throw up the window one spring
and the window weights break from their ropes
and fall deep in the wall.

AFTER MY GRANDMOTHER'S FUNERAL

After my grandmother's funeral,
as the dark river of mourners
murmured beneath me, I lay
on the floor of her attic,
watching the afternoon light
fade from the vault of old rafters
and dim to a film of gray dust
on her dresses and shoes.
I closed my eyes and slept,
but no dream came to me;
the coffin of that attic
was not to be borne aloft
on the good shoulders of cousins;
nor was it to roll on chrome wheels
to an altar with candles;
nor was I to awaken to find
my fingers laced loosely
over my heart. No dream came then
to help me leap over
the years to my death.
I awakened still young,
still sad, no longer welcome
in that darkening house.

A HOT NIGHT IN WHEAT COUNTRY

One doctor in a Piper Cub
can wake up everyone in North Dakota.

At the level of an open upstairs window,
a great white plain stretches away—
the naked Methodists
lying on top of their bedding.

The moon covers her eyes with a cloud.

FIVE P.M.

The pigeon flies to her resting place
on a window ledge above the traffic,
and her shadow, which cannot fly, climbs
swiftly over the bricks to meet her there.

Just so are you and I gathered at 5:00,
your bicycle left by the porch, the wind
still ringing in it, and my shoes by the bed,
still warm from walking home to you.

ABANDONED FARMHOUSE

He was a big man, says the size of his shoes
on a pile of broken dishes by the house;
a tall man too, says the length of the bed
in an upstairs room; and a good, God-fearing man,
says the Bible with a broken back
on the floor below the window, dusty with sun;
but not a man for farming, say the fields
cluttered with boulders and the leaky barn.

A woman lived with him, says the bedroom wall
papered with lilacs and the kitchen shelves
covered with oilcloth, and they had a child,
says the sandbox made from a tractor tire.
Money was scarce, say the jars of plum preserves
and canned tomatoes sealed in the cellar hole.
And the winters cold, say the rags in the window frames.
It was lonely here, says the narrow country road.

Something went wrong, says the empty house
in the weed-choked yard. Stones in the fields
say he was not a farmer; the still-sealed jars
in the cellar say she left in a nervous haste.
And the child? Its toys are strewn in the yard
like branches after a storm—a rubber cow,
a rusty tractor with a broken plow,
a doll in overalls. Something went wrong, they say.

THE BLIND ALWAYS COME
AS SUCH A SURPRISE

The blind always come as such a surprise,
suddenly filling an elevator
with a great white porcupine of canes,
or coming down upon us in a noisy crowd
like the eye of a hurricane.
The dashboards of cars stopped at crosswalks
and the shoes of commuters on trains
are covered with sentences
struck down in mid-flight by the canes of the blind.
Each of them changes our lives,
tapping across the bright circles of our ambitions
like cracks traversing the favorite china.

FURNACE

There's a click like a piece of chalk
tapping a blackboard, and the furnace
starts thinking: *Now, just where was I?*
It's always the same stale thought
turned over and over: *Got to
get something to eat.* Nothing else
ever enters its mind. After all,
it's a very old furnace,
and all of its friends have moved on.

WEST WINDOW

An owl
washes his claws
in the wind,
sets down
in light
no brighter
than a candle makes,
to eat. The days
draw back their warmth
from us
like cooling lamps.
We grow
to be alone
with table and cup.

BOARDING HOUSE

The blind man draws his curtains for the night
and goes to bed, leaving a burning light

above the bathroom mirror. Through the wall,
he hears the deaf man walking down the hall

in his squeaky shoes to see if there's a light
under the blind man's door, and all is right.

THE GEEK

Out back of the sideshow,
at dusk, the geek will be sitting
in freckles of light leaking out
of his tent, a hyena, eating
a hamburger out of a bag
and drinking a pint of warm port.
Over the onion-and-armpit smell
of the food may blow to him
clover and hay from a pasture
of cars, the smell of the sun
fading out of his tent, popcorn
and diesel oil and always, now
rising to him, the musty smell
of chickens, clucking in crates
under the blood-spattered stage
of his enterprise. Always he must
feel in his mouth their sharp skulls,
feel in his fingers their pulses,
always taste blood. He eats.
Watch now, as free for the asking
he swallows; see the bolus
of sustenance ball in his throat.

A LETTER FROM AUNT BELLE

You couldn't have heard about it there—
I'll send the clippings later on.

The afternoon that the neighbors' stove exploded—
how it reminded me of . . . Sarah's garden wedding!
Do you remember? It was beautiful.

As I was watering those slips
I promised you—the violets—
there was an awful thud, and Samson's wall
puffed up and blew the windows out.
It turned some pictures in the living room,
and that lovely vase you children gave to me
Christmas of '56 fell down, but I can glue it.

That Franklin boy you knew in school—
the one who got that girl in trouble—
ran in the Samson's house, but she was dead;
the blast collapsed her lungs, poor thing.
She always made me think of you,
but on the stretcher with her hair pinned up
and one old sandal off, she looked as old
as poor old me.
                    I have to go—
I've baked a little coffee cake
for Mr. Samson and the boys.

The violet slips are ready—
                              Write.

AT THE BAIT STAND

Part barn, part boxcar, part of a chicken shed,
part leaking water, something partly dead,
part pop machine, part gas pump, part a chair
leaned back against the wall, and sleeping there,
part-owner Herman Runner, mostly fat,
hip-waders, undershirt, tattoos and hat.

THE TATTOOED LADY

Around the smallpox vaccination scar
I'd hated since I was a little girl
I had him put this daisy, then its stem
because the flower looked too spidery
without a stem, and then these little leaves.
He said to think of it as just a gift
for a pretty girl. I went to him that night
because my arm was swollen, and I stayed
for twenty years. Around the daisy's stem
he slowly wound a snake that circled me
with swirls of trailer camps and cheap hotels
and sideshows, yet I loved the masterpiece
that I became to him. His touch had touched
me everywhere. His love is here to see.

A DEATH AT THE OFFICE

The news goes desk to desk
like a memo: *Initial
and pass on*. Each of us marks
Surprised or *Sorry*.

The management came early
and buried her nameplate
deep in her desk. They have boxed up
the Midol and Lip-Ice,

the snapshots from home,
wherever it was—nephews
and nieces, a strange, blurred cat
with fiery, flashbulb eyes

as if it grieved. But who grieves here?
We have her ballpoints back,
her bud vase. One of us tears
the scribbles from her calendar.

THERE IS ALWAYS A LITTLE WIND

There is always a little wind
in a country cemetery,
even on days when the air stands
still as a barn in the fields.

You can see the old cedars,
stringy and tough as maiden aunts,
taking the little gusts of wind
in their aprons like sheaves of wheat,

and hear above you the warm
and regular sweep of wheat being cut
and gathered, the wagons creaking,
the young men breathing at their work.

THE WIDOW LESTER

I was too old to be married,
but nobody told me.
I guess they didn't care enough.
How it had hurt, though, catching bouquets
all those years!
Then I met Ivan, and kept him,
and never knew love.
How his feet stunk in the bed sheets!
I could have told him to wash,
but I wanted to hold that stink against him.
The day he dropped dead in the field,
I was watching.
I was hanging up sheets in the yard,
and I finished.

HOUSES AT THE EDGE OF TOWN

These are the houses of farmers
retired from their fields;
white houses, freshly folded
and springing open again
like legal papers. These are houses
drawn up on the shore of the fields,
their nets still wet,
the fishermen sleeping curled in the bows.
See how the gardens
wade into the edge of the hayfield,
the cucumbers crawling out under the lilacs
to lie in the sun.

THE OLD WOMAN

The old woman, asleep on her back,
pulls up her knees and gives birth
to an empty house. She kicks off
the quilt and sheet and rakes her shift
up over her hips, showing her sex
to the photos of children
arranged on the opposite wall
who, years before, turned their
moonlit faces away.

A PLACE IN KANSAS

for Jon Gierlich

Somewhere in Kansas, a friend found
an empty stone house alone in a wheatfield.
Over the door was incised a ship's anchor.
There was no one to ask
what that anchor was doing in Kansas,
no water for miles.
Not a single white sail of a meaning
broke the horizon, though he stood there for hours.
It's like that in Kansas, forever.

TOM BALL'S BARN

for Bill Kloefkorn

The loan that built the barn
just wasn't big enough
to buy the paint, so the barn
went bare and fell apart
at the mortgaged end of twelve
nail-popping, splintering winters.
Besides the Januaries,
the barber says it was
five-and-a-half percent,
three dry years, seven wet,
and two indifferent,
the banker (dead five years),
and the bank (still open
but deaf, or *deef* as it were), *and*
poor iron in the nails that
were all to blame for the barn's collapse
on everything he owned, thus
leading poor Tom's good health
to diabetes and
the swollen leg that threw him
off the silo, probably
dead (the doctor said)
before he hit that board pile.

MY GRANDFATHER DYING

I could see bruises or shadows
deep under his skin, like the shapes
skaters find frozen in rivers—
leaves caught in flight,
or maybe the hand of a man reaching up
out of the darkness for help.

I was helpless as flowers
there at his bedside. I watched
his legs jerk in the sheets.
He answered doors,
he kicked loose stones from his fields.
I leaned down to call out my name
and he called it back. His breath
was as sour as an orchard
after the first frost.

THE RED WING CHURCH

There's a tractor in the doorway of a church
in Red Wing, Nebraska, in a coat of mud
and straw that drags the floor. A broken plow
sprawls beggarlike behind it on some planks
that make a sort of roadway up the steps.
The steeple's gone. A black tar-paper scar
that lightning might have made replaces it.
They've taken it down to change the house of God
to Homer Johnson's barn, but it's still a church,
with clumps of tiger lilies in the grass
and one of those boxlike, glassed-in signs
that give the sermon's topic (reading now
a bird's nest and a little broken glass).
The good works of the Lord are all around:
the steeple top is standing in a garden
just up the alley; it's a hen house now:
fat leghorns gossip at its crowded door.
Pews stretch on porches up and down the street,
the stained-glass windows style the mayor's house,
and the bell's atop the firehouse in the square.
The cross is only God knows where.

HIGHWAY 30

At two in the morning, when the moon
has driven away,
leaving the faint taillight of one star
at the horizon, a light
like moonlight leaks
from broken crates that lie fallen
along the highway, becoming
motels, all-night cafes, and bus stations
with greenhouse windows,
where lone women sit like overturned flowerpots,
crushing the soft, gray petals of old coats.

BIRTHDAY

Somebody deep in my bones
is lacing his shoes with a hook.
It's an hour before dawn
in that nursing home.
There is nothing to do but get dressed
and sit in the darkness.
Up the hall, in the brightly lit skull,
the young pastor is writing his poem.

THE FAILED SUICIDE

You have come back to us windblown
and wild-eyed, your fingertips numb
from squeezing the handle grips
of a four-day coma. Somehow,
out in that darkened countryside,
the road grew circular
and brought you back. We seem
another city, but the street signs
keep spelling your name, the same gnats
keep clouding the lights
high over the empty parking lots,
and the clock on the funeral home
(always a few minutes fast)
shines down upon a little fountain
where, nestled in curls of dead leaves,
a stone frog the color of your brain
prepares his leap.

A HAIRNET WITH STARS

I ate at the counter.
The waitress was wearing
a hairnet with stars,
pale blue stars
over the white clouds
of her hair, a woman
still lovely at sixty
or older, full breasted
and proud, her hands
strong and sensual,
smoothing the apron
over her belly.
I sighed and she turned
to me smiling.
"Mustard?" she asked.

THE GOLDFISH FLOATS
TO THE TOP OF HIS LIFE

The goldfish floats to the top of his life
and turns over, a shaving from somebody's hobby.
So it is that men die at the whims of great companies,
their neckties pulling them speechless into machines,
their wives finding them slumped in the shower,
their hearts blown open like boiler doors.
In the night, again and again these men float
to the tops of their dreams to drift back
to their desks in the morning. If you ask them,
they all would prefer to have died in their sleep.

THEY HAD TORN OFF MY FACE
AT THE OFFICE

They had torn off my face at the office.
The night that I finally noticed
that it was not growing back, I decided
to slit my wrists. Nothing ran out;
I was empty. Both of my hands fell off
shortly thereafter. Now at my job
they allow me to type with the stumps.
It pleases them to have helped me,
and I gain in speed and confidence.

A PRESIDENTIAL POEM

The president awakens in the night
and runs his fingers over the back of the land,
touching the vertebrae of rooftops,
laying his palm on the heartbeat
under the football fields.
                    Then, smaller,
the president lies naked beside us,
twisting a lock of our hair in his fingers,
scratching his belly. We awaken
in terror. At the heart of the house
we hear the refrigerator open and close,
then footfalls on the stairs. Soon
we learn to expect him. Every night,
at the foot of our beds in the darkness,
the president stands with his eyes upon us,
holding his breath.

YEAR'S END

Now the seasons are closing their files
on each of us, the heavy drawers
full of certificates rolling back
into the tree trunks, a few old papers
flocking away. Someone we loved
has fallen from our thoughts,
making a little, glittering splash
like a bicycle pushed by a breeze.
Otherwise, not much has happened;
we fell in love again, finding
that one red feather on the wind.

NEW YEAR'S DAY

Each thing in the clean morning light
is a promise. I start the day
by building a feeding place for the birds,
stacking up castaway crates in the snow.
How they come! Sparrows and blue jays
dropping like leaves from the elms,
which though burned with disease
still promise some sort of a spring,
their branches lined with hard buds
like birds perching, or the seeds of birds,
still more birds to come.

A DRY WINTER LETTER TO FRIENDS

Mid-January, and still no snow.
Out in the country, the junked cars
rust in their ditches, waiting
for beauty. Here in the city,
those toys that the children have given
to winter lie still in the leaves,
looking foolishly shiny. Each house
has a closet where huddle
the mourning galoshes, collapsing
with grief. I walk off to work
with dry feet and a zest for cold air
that's keen as a shovel.
For the past three years there's been
a blue canvas shoe in the bushes
out by the alley, a bright blue shoe
with a song in its heart. I read it as
an oracle: if we have snow this year,
it shall not bleed the color from our lives.

WALKING TO WORK

Today, it's the obsidian
ice on the sidewalk
with its milk white bubbles
popping under my shoes
that pleases me, and upon it
a lump of old snow
with a trail like a comet,
that somebody,
probably falling in love,
has kicked
all the way to the corner.

SUNDAY MORNING

Now it is June again, one of those
leafy Sundays drifting through galaxies
of maple seeds. Somewhere, a mourning dove
touches her keyboard twice, a lonely F,
and then falls silent. Here in the house
the Sunday papers lie in whitecaps
over the living-room floor. Among them floats
the bridal page, that window of many panes,
reflecting, black and white, patches of sky
and puffs of starlit cloud becoming
faces. On each bright brow the same light falls,
the nuptial moon held up just out of sight
to the left. The brides all lift their eyes
and smile to see the heavens stopped for them.
And love is everywhere. Cars that have all week
lurched and honked with sour commuters are now
like smooth canoes packed soft with families.
A church bell strides through the green perfume
of locust trees and tolls its thankfulness.
The mourning dove, to her astonishment,
blunders upon a distant call in answer.

ABOUT THE AUTHOR

TED KOOSER was born in Ames, Iowa, in 1939. He received his B.S. in English at Iowa State University and his M.A. in English at the University of Nebraska. His first collection of poems was published by University of Nebraska Press in 1969, and he has since published five collections of poems and several chapbooks. In addition to *Sure Signs, One World at a Time* has also been published in the Pitt Poetry Series. He has received two fellowships in poetry from the National Endowment for the Arts, the Society of Midland Authors poetry prize, the Stanley Kunitz Prize from *Columbia Magazine,* and two *Prairie Schooner*/Strousse Awards. Since 1964, he has made his living in the life insurance business and is currently an Associate Vice President of Lincoln Benefit Life Company in Lincoln, Nebraska.